United States
Department of
Agriculture

Forest Service

Southern
Research Station

Resource Bulletin
SRS-148

Fluctuations in National Forest Timber Harvest and Removals: The Southern Regional Perspective

Sonja N. Oswalt, Tony G. Johnson,
Mike Howell, and James W. Bentley

I0450446

The Authors:

Sonja N. Oswalt, Forester, **Tony G. Johnson,** Forester,
Mike Howell, Forester, and **James W. Bentley,** Forester,
U.S. Forest Service, Southern Research Station, Knoxville,
TN 37919.

Front cover:
Harvesting pine in Oklahoma. (photo by Tony G. Johnson)

May 2009

Southern Research Station
200 W.T. Weaver Blvd.
Asheville, NC 28804

Contents

Logging operation on national forests in Arkansas. (photo by Tony G. Johnson)

Fluctuations in National Forest Timber Harvest and Removals: The Southern Regional Perspective

Sonja N. Oswalt, Tony G. Johnson, Mike Howell, and James W. Bentley

Abstract

Here, we examine fluctuations in timber harvest and removals on National Forest System (NFS) lands of the Southern Region in light of changing societal values and administrative policies. We also present timber product utilization information based on multiple data sources, examine NFS removals in the context of standing volume, and compare NFS removals with removals on other ownerships. Additionally, we compare the estimates generated using the Forest Inventory and Analysis inventory with data collected and reported in the NFS Timber Cut and Sold reports. Data presented in this bulletin will enable NFS managers in the Southern Region to take a more indepth look at amounts of logging residue left on the ground versus merchantable material leaving the forest.

Keywords: FIA, logging residue, National Forest System, Region 8, removals, timber harvest, utilization.

Introduction

When established in 1905, the mission of the Forest Service, U.S. Department of Agriculture (USFS) and the system of public land that collectively comprised the National Forest System (NFS) was to ensure a continuous supply of clean water and timber for the U.S. population (Bergoffen 1976). Since its inception, goals and objectives of the Agency have changed with the needs and desires of the people it serves, coupled with new scientific knowledge and changing priorities in the American economy, political climate, and societal values. This became particularly true in 1960 with passage of the Multiple Use-Sustained Yield Act which officially broadened the Agency mission to include a variety of ecosystem functions beyond water and timber supply (Joyce and others 2008).

Attitudes toward NFS lands have shifted from thinking about public forests primarily as reservoirs of a viable timber supply to thinking about them as reservoirs for biodiversity, recreation, aesthetics, and other uses (Joyce and others 2008). In the early to mid-1990s, Forest Service Chief Dale Robertson introduced his "New Perspectives" plan for ecosystem management, which placed further emphasis on managing NFS lands to meet a variety of desired future conditions. The plan also called for an 80-percent reduction in clearcutting on NFS lands (Robertson 1992). In the 1980s and 1990s, the USFS revised its procedures for planning forest management, analyzing proposed actions, and involving the public in planning. New procedures were needed to meet requirements of the Endangered Species Act, National Forest Management Act, and the National Environmental Policy Act. During this period, NFS managers devoted more time and resources to analysis and documentation so that eventually, planning and analysis became principal activities (Bosworth and Brown 2007).

U.S. Forest Service employee Mike Howell instructs field personnel on the use of data recorders for logging operations before entering the woods in Florida. (photo by Tony G. Johnson)

Within most of the recently revised Southern Region Land and Resource Management Plans, harvests for the purpose of timber production and sale, once a primary function of the Nation's public forests, have become a minor component. Nonetheless, NFS lands still contribute to the timber supply and economy of the Southern States, and their contributions are infrequently studied within the context of the overall southern wood supply. Here, we examine timber harvest and removals on NFS lands in the Southern Region, considering changing societal values, administrative policies, and budget restrictions. We also present timber product utilization information based on multiple data sources, examine NFS timber removals in the context of standing volume, and compare NFS timber removals with other ownerships. Additionally, we compare estimates generated using the Forest Inventory and Analysis (FIA) inventory with data collected and reported in the NFS Timber Cut and Sold (NFS-CS) reports.

Methods

This study focused on the 13 Southern States inventoried by the USFS-FIA program, including Alabama, Arkansas, Florida, Georgia, Kentucky, Louisiana, Mississippi, North Carolina, Oklahoma, South Carolina, Tennessee, Texas, and Virginia. NFS Region 8, also known as the Southern Region, corresponds geographically with the southern FIA region. Southwide data related to forest land area and timberland area came from 2007 Resources Planning Act tables that were produced using the latest available FIA data at the time of table creation (available online at: http://www.fia.fs.fed.us/program-features/rpa/).

Two data sources were used to explore harvests and removals from NFS lands. The NFS is unique in that it maintains annual, publicly available NFS-CS reports for timber sales conducted on NFS lands (available online at: http://www.fs.fed.us/forestmanagement/reports/sold-harvest/index.shtml). These reports track the volume and value of timber sold, as well as the volume of timber that is cut, based on a presale cruise by USFS personnel, and any additions or subtractions that might occur during logging. Occasionally, sale units are defaulted and not cut. In such cases, the amount sold is greater than the amount cut. NFS-CS reports for Region 8 (excluding volume harvested on the George Washington National Forest and reported in West Virginia) were compiled and averaged for the years 1995 through 2006 to provide volumes harvested for that time period. Data from 1990 through 1994 were used to track trends in

Logger and forester discuss procedures on a harvesting operation in Oklahoma. (photo by Tony G. Johnson)

harvest levels, but were not used in further analysis. Prior to 2001, cubic foot volumes were not reported in NFS-CS reports. A factor of 5.5 board feet was used for all cubic foot volumes reported from 1990 to 2000. Beginning in 2001, the NFS reported volumes in cubic feet. Thus, comparisons of conversion factors in this report will produce slightly different estimates.

FIA estimates of volume and removals for all ownerships were generated using the most current estimates of all-live and growing-stock standing volume and all-live removals for the 13 Southern States (U.S. Department of Agriculture 2007). Data collection timeframes ranged from 1990 through 2006 based on the date of each State's most recent inventory.

The FIA sample on NFS includes a relatively small number of inventory plots, and estimates may differ significantly from harvest volumes reported in individual NFS-CS reports. In addition, removals from all inventory plots include volume that is cut and not utilized for a product, logging residues, and standing volume reclassified to a reserved status or to another land use change. The removal values generated by FIA represent an approximate average annual value for the years 1995 through 2006, and represent broad estimates only. Though less accurate than the NFS-CS reports, the removals data collected by FIA can be used in conjunction with other FIA data in a more seamless fashion.

In addition, felled-tree utilization studies are conducted across the South to determine underutilization factors that are applied to the removals volume. These studies are used to refine the logging residue estimates. The most current studies show that about 95 percent of the merchantable bole for softwoods is utilized, while 87 percent of the merchantable hardwood bole is actually utilized for products (Bentley and Johnson 2006). The merchantable portion is defined as the portion of live trees ≥ 5.0 inches diameter at breast height (d.b.h.) between a 1-foot stump and a minimum 4.0-inch top on the central stem. Volume defined as utilized for products was therefore determined by adjusting the merchantable utilized volume by these known percentages in order to account for underutilization.

Implications and Discussion

National Forest System and the Southern Landscape

Southern forests occupied 215 million acres on the landscape and supported 326 billion cubic feet of timber, 89 percent of which was growing stock (tables A.1 and A.3). National forests occupied 6 percent of the total southern forest area, 6 percent of timberland area (table A.2, fig. 1), and they accounted for about 9 percent of the standing-live and growing-stock volume on timberland. Standing-live

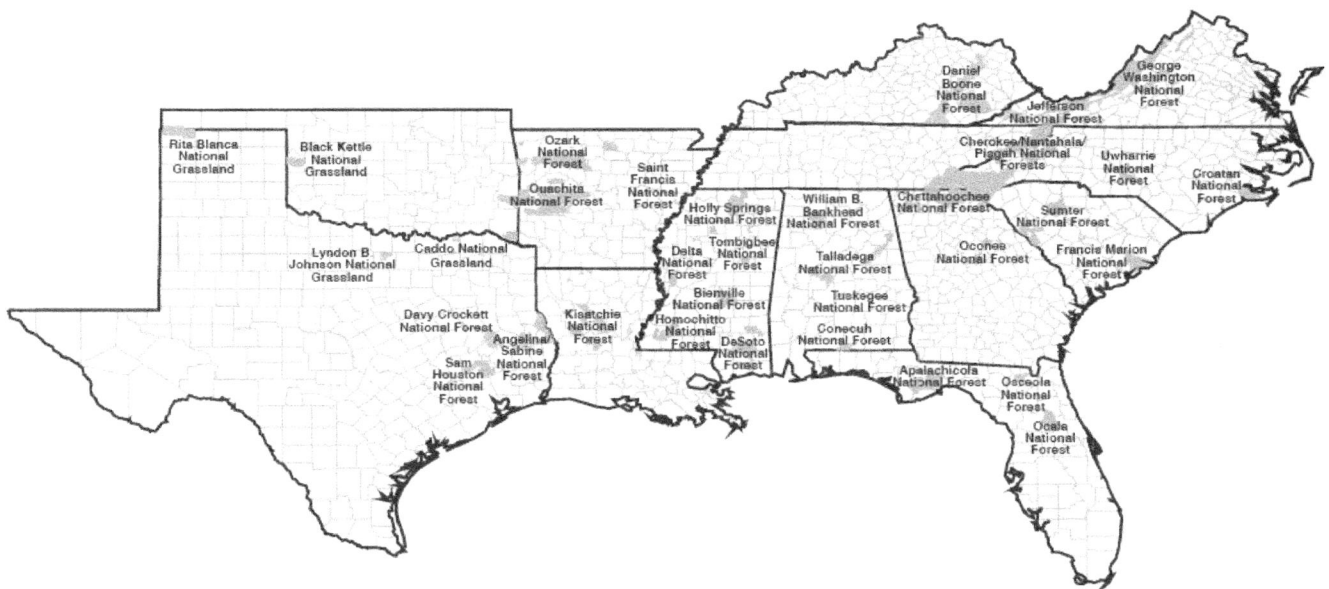

Figure 1—National Forest System lands in the South.

volume on NFS timberland for softwood and hardwood combined was 28 billion cubic feet, and growing-stock volume totaled 25 billion cubic feet (tables A.3 and A.4). To put that in perspective, standing-live volume on all NFS timberland in the South is roughly equal to the standing-live volume on timberland in the entire State of Arkansas, or seven times the standing-live volume on timberland in the State of Oklahoma. Although NFS timberland occupies a seemingly small proportion of the southern landscape, it clearly remains an important component of the southern forest resource.

National Forest System Harvest and Sales in the Southern Region

Southern NFS-CS reports for 1995 through 2006 showed an average annual harvest of >93.6 million cubic feet (508.6 million board feet) (table A.5). Volume cut and sold on NFS land from 1995 through 2006 ranged from 50.7 million cubic feet (278.8 million board feet) in 2003 to 153.8 million cubic feet (846.0 million board feet) in 1996. Harvest volume averaged 125.4 million cubic feet from 1995 through 1999 and then dropped to an average of just 70.9 million cubic feet from 2000 through 2006. Overall, from 1990 through 2005, harvest volume on NFS land declined 74 percent from 257.8 million cubic feet to 66.1 million cubic feet (fig. 2). This overall downward trend in harvests reflects the increased involvement of the Agency in

revisions of land management plans and associated appeals and litigation, as well as reductions in overall operating budgets. Harvest volume experienced an upswing in 2006 to 129.0 million cubic feet; still 50 percent less than the 1990 NFS harvest. This upswing occurred right after Hurricanes Katrina and Rita pummeled the coastline of the Gulf States. Most of the increase can be attributed to harvests and salvage logging that occurred in response to the catastrophic storms. Harvesting on national forests in Mississippi jumped from 11.9 million cubic feet in 2005 to 58.4 million cubic feet in 2006 (table A.14), while harvests on national forests in Texas increased from 4.6 million cubic feet in 2005 to 11.6 million cubic feet in 2006 (table A.19).

Between 1995 and 2006, revenues generated from harvest sales on NFS land totaled >$798.4 million, or an average of $66.5 million per year (table A.5). This amounted to an average of $131.12 per thousand board feet over the period. Softwoods accounted for 85 percent of total volume harvested and sold (79.4 million cubic feet), while hardwoods accounted for the remaining 15 percent (14.2 million cubic feet) (table A.6).

Average annual volume harvested as sawtimber for saw logs processed into lumber and veneer products totaled 54.6 million cubic feet (296.0 million board feet) and accounted for 58 percent of harvest (tables A.6 and A.7). Softwood sawtimber made up 88 percent, or 47.9 million cubic feet,

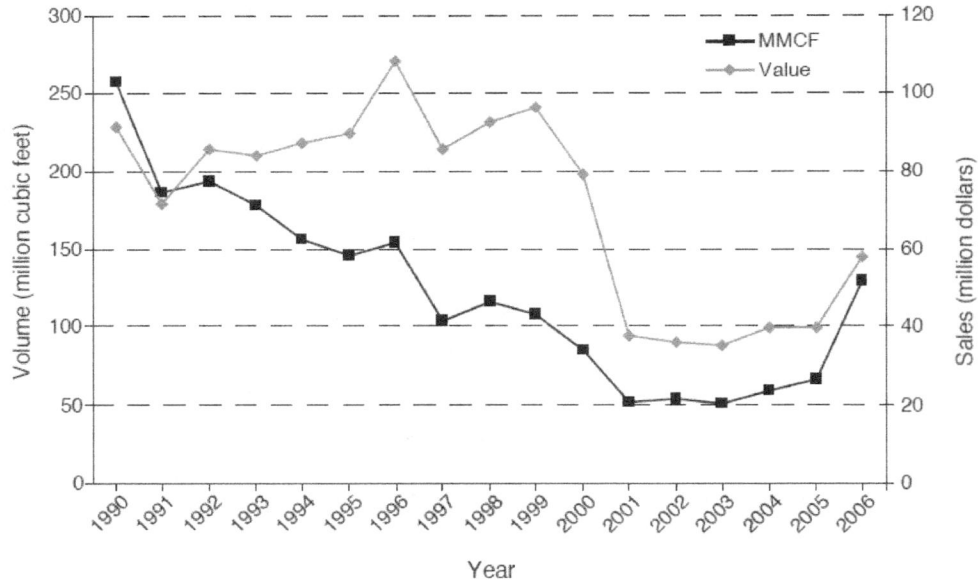

Figure 2—Annual harvests and sales on National Forest System land, 1990–2006.

Log landing at harvest operation in Arkansas. (photo by Tony G. Johnson)

while hardwood volume accounted for the remaining 12 percent, or 6.7 million cubic feet. Volume sold for pulpwood totaled 37.2 million cubic feet (202.7 million board feet) and accounted for 40 percent of harvest. At 31.1 million cubic feet, softwood accounted for 84 percent of the pulpwood harvested. Domestic firewood cut on southern NFS land amounted to 1.4 million cubic feet, or about 2 percent of total harvest volume. Most of the volume harvested for firewood was hardwood.

Tables A.8 through A.20 provide individual State level NFS-CS reports for the years 1990 to 2006. We analyzed 1995 to 2006 data in order to coincide with FIA removals data periods. For those years, the NFS-CS reports indicate that 50 percent of the volume harvested on southern NFS land came from Arkansas and Mississippi. Therefore, one-half the total harvest volume came from 30 percent of the land base (table A.1). When combined, these States accounted for an average of $37.3 million, or 56 percent, of total dollars generated from sales, annually.

Forest Inventory and Analysis—Removals

FIA inventory data from 1995 through 2006 showed that total average annual removals of all live trees across all ownerships in the South equaled 11.2 billion cubic feet, of which 61 percent was softwood and 39 percent was hardwood (table A.21). About 86 percent of live-tree removal volume Southwide was considered by FIA inventory crews to have been utilized. Across all ownerships in the South, Georgia, Alabama, and North Carolina accounted for the highest proportion of total all-live removals, with 14 percent, 12 percent, and 11 percent of the Southwide total, respectively.

Between 1995 and 2006, FIA inventory data showed that average annual all-live removals from the South's national forests totaled 178.9 million cubic feet (715.6 million board feet of sawtimber), or 0.7 percent of the standing all-live volume on southern NFS land per year (table A.22). As stated earlier, removals from inventory data include volume utilized for products, volume left unutilized as logging residue, and volume reclassified to a reserved status or another land use such as campgrounds.

Volume classified as utilized on southern NFS lands by FIA inventory crews totaled 109.2 million cubic feet for softwoods and hardwoods combined. This volume is reported from a 1-foot stump to a 4-inch top. Felled-tree utilization studies conducted across the South show that about 95 percent of the merchantable softwood bole is utilized for products, while 87 percent of the merchantable hardwood bole is utilized. Therefore, the remainder of FIA-derived removals, described below, have been adjusted. With this in mind, the utilized volume was adjusted to 102.3 million cubic feet utilized for products to account for underutilization. Of this volume, 77.1 million cubic feet (75 percent) was softwood volume and 25.1 million cubic feet (25 percent) was hardwood volume.

Unutilized volume due to logging residues totaled 21.2 million cubic feet, or 12 percent of total southern NFS removals. Softwoods accounted for 9.9 million cubic feet (47 percent), while hardwoods accounted for 11.3 million cubic feet (53 percent) of logging residue. Volume removed as a result of reclassification (e.g., reclassified from timberland to reserved land) totaled 55.4 million cubic feet, or 31 percent of total all-live removals and about 72 percent of all

Tombigbee National Forest in Mississippi. (photo by Sonja N. Oswalt)

nonutilized wood. Hardwoods accounted for 68 percent, or 37.6 million cubic feet of removals due to reclassifications.

The difference between total FIA inventory removals (178.9 million cubic feet) and the 93.6 million cubic feet reported in the NFS-CS reports was attributed to: (1) unutilized material in the form of logging residues (21.2 million cubic feet), (2) volume reclassified to another land use or as reserved (55.4 million cubic feet), and (3) error rates associated with FIA removals data (8.7 million cubic feet). The statistical error for total all-live removals on national forests is ± 23 percent at a 99 percent confidence level, which means that we are 99 percent certain that the true volume of all removals from NFS lands falls between 137.8 and 220.0 million cubic feet. Assuming that the error rate is similar for adjusted utilized removals on southern NFS land, values would fall between 78.8 and 125.8 million cubic feet, well within the range of NFS-CS values.

National forests in Mississippi and Arkansas accounted for the largest proportion of southern NFS removals recorded by FIA, with 24 percent and 23 percent of all-live removals, respectively. Softwood volume comprised the majority of removals on NFS land in most southern-tier States such as Alabama, Arkansas, Florida, Louisiana, Mississippi, South Carolina, and Texas. Conversely, hardwood volume comprised the majority of removals on the mountainous NFS lands of Georgia, Kentucky, North Carolina, Tennessee, and Virginia. National forest land accounted for 2 percent of all-live removals, Southwide.

Removals on Other Ownerships

In the South, other public lands such as national, State, or local parks and forests accounted for 7 percent of forest land area, 6 percent of timberland area, and about 8 percent of timberland growing-stock standing volume. Total all-live tree removals on other public lands equaled about 430 million cubic feet, or 4 percent of all-live tree removals (table A.23). That amounts to more than twice as much volume compared to NFS land, even though the timberland area available for harvest is nearly the same. Like NFS removals, 57 percent of removals on other public lands were utilized, and the majority of unutilized material was hardwood. Seventy-three percent of all live utilized removals on other public land came from softwoods.

Forest industry, or private corporate ownerships, made up about 28 percent of timberland area in the South, and accounted for 22 percent of total all-live tree removals (tables A.2 and A.24). Only about 5 percent of industrial removals were not utilized, and the unutilized material was split about evenly between softwood and hardwood material.

Logging residue following a mixed-species harvest in Georgia. (photo by Tony G. Johnson)

Eighty-two percent of industrial all-live tree removals were softwood species.

Nonindustrial private forest land (NIPF) made up 60 percent of southern forest land and timberland area, and accounted for 72 percent of all-live tree removals (tables A.1 and A.25). About 15 percent of removals on NIPF were not utilized. Seventy-three percent of unutilized material was hardwood, while 56 percent of utilized material was softwood. Georgia, Alabama, North Carolina, and Mississippi had the highest NIPF removals volumes, for the period studied.

Conclusions

The NFS was originally designated as a continuing source of timber for the United States. Since its inception, however, the mission of the NFS has evolved to represent the changing needs of the Nation, and the desires of its people. The NFS mission was particularly changed by the environmental

movements that began in the mid-1970s and continue to the present. The effect of changing NFS values is apparent in the South when examining the large decrease in harvest volumes from 1990 through 2006. The decline in harvesting on southern NFS land becomes even more noticeable when compared with harvest levels on other public lands (e.g., U.S. Fish and Wildlife Service land, State parks, etc.), which comprise a similar land area, but harvested nearly 2.5 times as much material during the period studied.

This study illustrates the compatibility of FIA removal volumes with NFS-CS reports. However, the reader should keep in mind that direct comparison of any individual NFS-CS report year with average annual removal estimates from FIA data are not valid and could lead to erroneous conclusions. One benefit of being able to confirm the compatibility between the NFS-CS reports and FIA removals data is the subsequent ability to segment FIA removals data into utilized and nonutilized material based on FIA crew determinations and to refine logging residue estimates based on timber utilization studies conducted in the South. Data presented here will enable NFS managers Southwide to: (1) better evaluate the effects of forest land being converted to other land uses, (2) quantify the volume of wood being left on-the-ground in the form of logging residue, and (3) assess the volume of wood leaving the forest as merchantable material. In a time when available post-harvest biomass is raising interest throughout the United States, this data is particularly relevant and important.

Acknowledgments

The authors gratefully acknowledge Carolyn Steppleton for her hard work within the Resource Use Section of FIA, and Helen Beresford for her hard work developing the Timber Product Output tablemaker. Additionally, we thank the reviewers of this bulletin for their careful attention. Your reviews have greatly improved the bulletin.

Literature Cited

Bentley, J.W.; Johnson, T.G. 2006. North Carolina harvest and utilization study, 2002. Resour. Bull. SRS–109. Asheville, NC: U.S. Department of Agriculture Forest Service, Southern Research Station. 23 p.

Bergoffen, W.W. 1976. 100 years of federal forestry. Agric. Info. Bull. No. 402. Washington, DC: U.S. Department of Agriculture Forest Service. [Not paged].

Bosworth, D.; Brown, H. 2007. After the timber wars: community-based stewardship. Journal of Forestry. 105(5): 271–273.

Joyce, L.A.; Blate, G.M.; Littell, J.S. [and others]. 2008. National forests. In: Julius, S.H.; West, J.M., eds. Preliminary review of adaptation options for climate-sensitive ecosystems and resources. Final report, synthesis and assessment product 4.4. Washington, DC: U.S. Environmental Protection Agency, Climate Change Science Program: 3–1 to 3–127.

Robertson, F.D. 1992. Statement of F. Dale Robertson, Chief, Forest Service U.S. Department of Agriculture before the Subcommittee on Forests, Family Farms, and Energy, committee on Agriculture, United States House of Representatives. http://fs.jorge.com/archives/History_National/ClearcuttingRoberston1992.htm. [Date accessed: September 30, 2008].

U.S. Department of Agriculture Forest Service. 2007. Forest inventory and analysis national core field guide. Version 4.0. http://srsfia2.fs.fed.us/data_acquisition/field_guide.shtml. [Date accessed: September 30, 2008].

Residual biomass after a hardwood removal in Georgia. (photo by Tony G. Johnson)

Glossary

Board foot. Unit of measure applied to roundwood. It relates to lumber that is 1-foot long, 1-foot wide, and 1-inch thick (or its equivalent).

Composite products. Roundwood products manufactured into chips, wafers, strands, flakes, shavings, or sawdust and then reconstituted into a variety of panel and engineered lumber products.

Domestic fuelwood. The volume of roundwood harvested to produce heat for residential settings.

Drain. The volume of roundwood removed from any geographic area where timber is grown.

Growing-stock removals. The growing-stock volume removed from poletimber and sawtimber trees in the timberland inventory. (Note: Includes volume removed for roundwood products, logging residues, and other removals.)

Growing-stock trees. Living trees of commercial species classified as sawtimber, poletimber, saplings, and seedlings. Growing-stock trees must contain at least one 12-foot or two 8-foot logs in the saw-log portion, currently or potentially (if too small to qualify). The log(s) must meet dimension and merchantability standards and have, currently or potentially, one-third of the gross board-foot volume in sound wood.

Growing-stock volume. The cubic-foot volume of sound wood in growing-stock trees at least 5.0 inches d.b.h. from a 1-foot stump to a minimum 4.0-inch top d.o.b. of the central stem.

Hardwoods. Dicotyledonous trees, usually broadleaf and deciduous.

Soft hardwoods. Hardwood species such as gum, yellow-poplar, cottonwood, red maple, basswood, or willow, that have an average specific gravity of ≤0.50.

Hard hardwoods. Hardwood species such as oak, hard maple, hickory, or beech, that have an average specific gravity >0.50.

Industrial roundwood products. Any primary use of the main stem of a tree, such as saw logs, pulpwood, and veneer logs, intended to be processed into primary wood products, such as lumber, wood pulp, and sheathing, at primary wood-using mills.

International ¼-inch rule. A log rule or formula for estimating the board-foot volume of logs, allowing ½-inch of taper for each 4-foot length. The rule appears in a number of forms that allow for kerf (saw-blade width). In the form used by FIA, ¼-inch of kerf is assumed. This rule is used as the USDA Forest Service standard log rule in the Eastern United States.

Log. A primary forest product harvested in long, primarily 8-, 12-, and 16-foot lengths.

Logging residues. The unused portion(s) of live trees cut or destroyed during logging operations.

Merchantable portion (bole length). That portion of live trees ≥5.0 inches d.b.h. between a 1-foot stump and a minimum 4.0-inch top d.o.b. on the central stem. That portion of primary forks from the point of occurrence to a minimum 4.0-inch top d.o.b. is included.

Merchantable volume. Solid-wood volume in the merchantable portion of live trees.

Noncommercial species. Tree species of typically small size, poor form, or inferior quality that normally do not develop into trees suitable for industrial wood products.

Nonforest land. Land that has never supported forests or land formerly forested where timber production is precluded by development for other uses.

Nongrowing-stock sources. The net volume removed from the nongrowing-stock portions of poletimber and sawtimber trees (stumps, tops, limbs, cull sections of central stem) and from any portion of a rough, rotten, sapling, dead, or nonforest tree.

Other forest land. Forest land other than timberland and productive reserved forest land. It includes available and reserved forest land that is incapable of annually producing 20 cubic feet per acre of industrial wood under natural conditions because of adverse site conditions such as sterile soils, dry climate, poor drainage, high elevation, steepness, or rockiness.

Other products. A miscellaneous category of roundwood products, e.g., cooperage, excelsior, shingles, and mill residue byproducts (charcoal, bedding, mulch, etc.).

Other removals. The growing-stock volume of trees removed from the inventory by cultural operations such as timber stand improvement, land clearing, and other changes in land use, resulting in the removal of the trees from timberland.

Other sources. (See: Nongrowing-stock sources.)

Posts, poles, and pilings. Roundwood products milled (cut or peeled) into standard sizes (lengths and circumferences) to be put in the ground to provide vertical and lateral support in buildings, foundations, utility lines, and fences. May also include nonindustrial (unmilled) products.

Poletimber-size trees. Softwoods 5.0 to 8.9 inches d.b.h. and hardwoods 5.0 to 10.9 inches d.b.h.

Primary wood-using plants. Industries that convert round-wood products (saw logs, veneer logs, pulpwood, etc.) into primary wood products, such as lumber, veneer or sheathing, and wood pulp.

Pulpwood. A roundwood product that will be reduced to individual wood fibers by chemical or mechanical means. The fibers are used to make a broad generic group of pulp products that includes paper products, as well as chipboard, fiberboard, insulating board, and paperboard.

Rotten trees. Live trees of commercial species not containing at least one 12-foot saw log, or two noncontiguous saw logs, each 8 feet or longer, now or prospectively, primarily because of rot or missing sections, and with less than one-third of the gross board-foot tree volume in sound material.

Rough trees. Live trees of commercial species not containing at least one 12-foot saw log, or two noncontiguous saw logs, each 8 feet or longer, now or prospectively, primarily because of roughness, poor form, splits, and cracks, and with less than one-third of the gross board-foot tree volume in sound material; and live trees of noncommercial species.

Roundwood (roundwood logs). Logs, bolts, or other round sections cut from trees for industrial manufacture or consumer uses.

Roundwood chipped. Any timber cut primarily for industrial manufacture, delivered to nonpulpmills, chipped, and then sold to pulpmills for use as fiber. Includes tops, jump sections, whole trees, and pulpwood sticks.

Roundwood products. Any primary product, such as lumber, poles, pilings, pulp, or fuelwood that is produced from roundwood.

Roundwood product drain. That portion of total drain used for a product.

Salvable dead trees. Standing or downed dead trees that were formerly growing stock and considered merchantable. Trees must be at least 5.0 inches d.b.h. to qualify.

Saplings. Live trees 1.0 to 5.0 inches d.b.h.

Saw log. A roundwood product, usually 8 feet in length or longer, processed into a variety of sawn products such as lumber, cants, pallets, railroad ties, and timbers.

Saw-log portion. The part of the bole of sawtimber trees between a 1-foot stump and the saw-log top.

Saw-log top. The point on the bole of sawtimber trees above which a conventional saw log cannot be produced. The minimum saw-log top is 7.0 inches d.o.b. for softwoods and 9.0 inches d.o.b. for hardwoods.

Sawtimber-size trees. Softwoods ≥ 9.0 inches d.b.h. and hardwoods ≥ 11.0 inches d.b.h.

Sawtimber volume. Growing-stock volume in the saw-log portion of sawtimber-sized trees in board feet (International ¼-inch rule).

Seedlings. Trees < 1.0 inch d.b.h. and ≥ 1 foot tall for hardwoods, ≥ 6 inches tall for softwood, and > 0.5 inch in diameter at ground level for longleaf pine.

Softwoods. Coniferous trees, usually evergreen, having leaves that are needles or scalelike.

Standard cord. A unit of measure applied to roundwood, usually bolts or split wood. It is a stack of wood 4 feet high, 4 feet wide, and 8 feet long encompassing 128 cubic feet of wood, bark, and air space. This usually translates to approximately 75.0 to 81.0 cubic feet of solid wood for pulpwood, because pulpwood is more uniform.

Standard unit. A unit measure applied to roundwood timber products. Board feet (International ¼-inch rule) is the standard unit used for saw logs and veneer; cords are used for pulpwood, composite panel, and fuelwood; hundred pieces for poles; thousand pieces for posts; and thousand cubic feet for all other miscellaneous forest products.

Timberland. Forest land capable of producing 20 cubic feet of industrial wood per acre per year and not withdrawn from timber utilization.

Timber products. Roundwood products and byproducts.

Timber product output. The total volume of roundwood products from all sources plus the volume of byproducts recovered from mill residues (equals roundwood product drain).

Timber removals. The total volume of trees removed from the timberland inventory by harvesting, cultural operations such as stand improvement, land clearing, or changes in land use. (Note: Includes roundwood products, logging residues, and other removals.)

Tree. Woody plant having one erect perennial stem or trunk at least 3 inches d.b.h., a more or less definitely formed crown of foliage, and a height of at least 13 feet (at maturity).

Upper-stem portion. The part of the main stem of sawtimber trees above the saw-log top and the minimum top diameter of 4.0 inches outside bark, or to the point where the main stem breaks into limbs.

Utilization studies. Studies conducted on active logging operations to develop factors for merchantable portions of trees left in the woods (logging residues), logging damage, and utilization of the unmerchantable portion of growing-stock trees and nongrowing-stock trees.

Veneer log. A roundwood product either rotary cut, sliced, stamped, or sawn into a variety of veneer products such as plywood, finished panels, veneer sheets, or sheathing.

Weight. A unit of measure for mill residues, expressed as oven-dry tons (2,000 oven-dry pounds).

Appendix

Index of Tables

Table A.1—Forest land area in the Southern United States by State and ownership, 2007

State	All owner-ships	Public						Private		
		Total public	Federal			State	County and municipal	Total private	Private corporate	Private non-corporate
			Total Federal	National forest	Other					
					thousand acres					
Alabama	22,693	1,429	986	746	240	330	113	21,264	6,311	14,953
Arkansas	18,830	3,674	3,155	2,546	609	448	71	15,156	5,454	9,703
Florida	16,147	4,720	2,068	1,067	1,000	2,221	431	11,427	6,441	4,986
Georgia	24,784	2,343	1,758	736	1,022	356	230	22,440	7,965	14,475
Kentucky	11,970	1,324	1,059	744	315	212	53	10,647	1,491	9,156
Louisiana	14,222	1,709	975	695	279	538	197	12,512	6,499	6,014
Mississippi	19,622	2,303	1,834	1,326	508	236	233	17,320	4,714	12,605
North Carolina	18,447	2,950	2,090	1,169	921	601	258	15,497	3,882	11,615
Oklahoma	7,665	665	499	245	255	139	27	7,000	1,283	5,716
South Carolina	12,746	1,557	1,071	641	430	325	160	11,189	3,574	7,615
Tennessee	14,480	2,171	1,473	741	732	599	99	12,310	2,209	10,101
Texas	17,273	1,069	905	682	224	109	54	16,204	4,418	11,786
Virginia	15,766	2,766	2,250	1,692	558	302	213	13,000	2,912	10,088
Total	214,644	28,679	20,124	13,031	7,093	6,417	2,139	185,965	57,153	128,812

Source: 2007 Resources Planning Act.

Table A.2—Timberland area in the Southern United States by State and ownership group, 2007

State	All owners	Ownership group			
		National forest	Other public	Private corporate	Private non-corporate
		thousand acres			
Alabama	22,581	687	637	6,311	14,946
Arkansas	18,479	2,440	985	5,447	9,607
Florida	15,552	1,029	3,136	6,409	4,978
Georgia	24,247	612	1,208	7,959	14,468
Kentucky	11,648	590	440	1,472	9,146
Louisiana	14,116	672	953	6,477	6,014
Mississippi	19,535	1,316	936	4,713	12,570
North Carolina	17,917	1,093	1,388	3,866	11,570
Oklahoma	6,233	223	359	1,257	4,394
South Carolina	12,641	619	838	3,569	7,615
Tennessee	13,913	666	937	2,209	10,101
Texas	11,859	662	293	4,404	6,500
Virginia	15,309	1,616	709	2,908	10,076
Total	204,030	12,225	12,819	57,001	121,985

Source: 2007 Resources Planning Act.

Table A.3—Net volume of live trees on timberland in the Southern United States by State and ownership group, 2007

State	All owners	Ownership group		
		National forest	Other public	Total private
		million cubic feet		
Alabama	32,264	1,440	1,339	29,485
Arkansas	27,103	4,360	2,335	20,408
Florida	18,936	1,227	4,695	13,013
Georgia	38,290	1,761	2,576	33,953
Kentucky	21,286	1,403	984	18,899
Louisiana	22,262	1,866	2,105	18,291
Mississippi	29,510	3,336	1,767	24,408
North Carolina	35,392	3,168	2,771	29,453
Oklahoma	3,914	328	300	3,286
South Carolina	21,481	1,347	1,965	18,169
Tennessee	26,573	1,810	2,211	22,552
Texas	17,228	2,127	533	14,569
Virginia	31,699	3,621	1,769	26,309
Total	325,936	27,793	25,350	272,794

Table A.4—Net volume of growing stock on timberland in the Southern United States by State and ownership group, 2007

State	All owners	Ownership group		
		National forest	Other public	Total private
		million cubic feet		
Alabama	28,569	1,332	1,210	26,027
Arkansas	24,658	4,009	2,144	18,504
Florida	16,603	1,110	4,935	10,558
Georgia	34,390	1,557	2,325	30,507
Kentucky	18,301	1,302	852	16,148
Louisiana	20,500	1,795	1,887	16,818
Mississippi	26,049	3,120	1,548	21,381
North Carolina	32,777	2,931	2,573	27,274
Oklahoma	3,001	294	225	2,482
South Carolina	19,163	1,240	1,768	16,155
Tennessee	22,910	1,622	1,976	19,313
Texas	16,000	2,093	487	13,421
Virginia	26,881	2,854	1,536	22,492
Total	289,803	25,258	23,465	241,080

Table A.5—Timber cut and sold on southern national forests, 1990 to 2006

Year	Volume		Value	
	thousand board feet	*thousand cubic feet*	*dollars*	*dollars per thousand board feet*
1990	1,418,166	257,848	91,601,985.29	64.59
1991	1,025,236	186,407	71,486,191.23	69.73
1992	1,061,478	192,996	85,683,527.47	80.72
1993	977,043	177,644	84,066,132.33	86.04
1994	860,219	156,404	87,401,722.53	101.60
1995	804,128	146,205	89,842,295.16	111.73
1996	846,041	153,826	108,317,341.72	128.03
1997	571,124	103,841	85,689,748.84	150.04
1998	635,583	115,561	92,522,181.62	145.57
1999	592,988	107,816	96,512,798.55	162.76
2000	467,827	85,059	78,956,974.37	168.77
2001	285,780	52,191	37,531,471.04	131.33
2002	294,427	53,534	36,021,529.39	122.34
2003	278,758	50,707	35,259,585.34	126.49
2004	323,573	59,365	39,835,634.25	123.11
2005	347,535	66,123	39,889,343.08	114.78
2006	655,544	129,043	57,996,402.94	88.47
Total[a]	6,103,308	1,123,270	798,375,306.30	
Average[a]	508,609	93,606	66,531,275.53	131.12

[a] The years 1995 to 2006 were used for total and average volume harvested.

Table A.6—Timber cut and sold on southern national forests by product and species group, 1990 to 2006

Year	All products Total	Soft-wood	Hard-wood	Sawtimber Total	Soft-wood	Hard-wood	Pulpwood Total	Soft-wood	Hard-wood	Fuelwood Total	Soft-wood	Hard-wood	Miscellaneous products Total	Soft-wood	Hard-wood
							thousand cubic feet								
1990	257,848	214,243	43,605	145,039	127,718	17,321	108,001	86,473	21,528	4,758	38	4,720	50	14	36
1991	186,407	145,910	40,497	94,570	78,410	16,161	87,408	67,369	20,039	4,080	58	4,022	348	72	275
1992	192,996	152,580	40,416	100,687	84,717	15,970	88,020	67,735	20,285	4,178	51	4,127	112	76	35
1993	177,644	139,729	37,915	85,695	71,047	14,647	86,996	68,004	18,992	4,277	28	4,249	676	649	27
1994	156,404	126,396	30,008	75,445	64,242	11,203	77,064	61,709	15,354	3,506	65	3,440	390	379	11
1995	146,205	122,247	23,958	72,591	63,281	9,309	70,450	58,591	11,859	2,829	56	2,773	335	319	16
1996	153,826	130,202	23,624	86,476	75,484	10,993	64,692	53,974	10,718	1,946	39	1,906	711	705	7
1997	103,841	84,151	19,689	61,991	52,037	9,954	39,980	31,914	8,067	1,678	15	1,663	191	185	6
1998	115,561	97,578	17,983	68,461	59,395	9,066	45,261	37,786	7,475	1,439	12	1,427	399	384	15
1999	107,816	91,762	16,054	63,683	56,262	7,421	42,869	35,201	7,668	954	5	949	309	295	15
2000	85,059	71,097	13,963	48,676	42,246	6,430	34,778	28,373	6,405	1,037	1	1,036	569	477	93
2001	52,191	44,375	7,816	29,561	26,124	3,437	21,500	18,052	3,448	917	2	915	213	198	15
2002	53,534	47,099	6,435	30,451	27,824	2,627	21,982	19,165	2,817	870	11	860	231	100	131
2003	50,707	42,106	8,600	28,773	23,900	4,874	20,566	18,125	2,441	1,278	3	1,275	89	79	11
2004	59,366	48,908	10,457	35,339	30,154	5,185	22,676	18,687	3,989	1,239	1	1,237	112	66	46
2005	66,123	55,382	10,741	37,344	31,784	5,561	27,444	23,496	3,948	1,217	1	1,216	117	101	16
2006	129,043	117,731	11,312	91,474	86,098	5,376	34,068	29,639	4,430	1,463	3	1,460	2,038	1,991	47
Total[a]	1,123,270	952,639	170,631	654,820	574,588	80,232	446,268	373,002	73,266	16,868	151	16,717	5,314	4,898	416
Average[a]	93,606	79,387	14,219	54,568	47,882	6,686	37,189	31,084	6,106	1,406	13	1,393	443	408	35

[a] The years 1995 to 2006 were used for total and average volume harvested.

Table A.7—Timber cut and sold on southern national forests by product and species group, 1990 to 2006

Year	All products			Sawtimber			Pulpwood			Fuelwood			Miscellaneous products		
	Total	Soft-wood	Hard-wood	Total	Soft-wood	Hard-wood	Total	Soft-wood	Hard-wood	Total	Soft-wood	Hard-wood	Total	Soft-wood	Hard-wood
							thousand board feet								
1990	1,418,166	1,178,339	239,827	797,716	702,450	95,266	594,005	475,602	118,403	26,169	208	25,961	276	79	196
1991	1,025,236	802,502	222,734	520,138	431,254	88,884	480,746	370,531	110,215	22,440	319	22,120	1,913	399	1,515
1992	1,061,478	839,188	222,290	553,778	465,945	87,833	484,110	372,542	111,568	22,976	280	22,696	614	420	193
1993	977,043	768,509	208,534	471,320	390,760	80,559	478,480	374,021	104,458	23,526	156	23,370	3,717	3,571	146
1994	860,219	695,176	165,043	414,946	353,331	61,615	423,850	339,402	84,448	19,281	359	18,922	2,143	2,084	59
1995	804,128	672,360	131,769	399,248	348,047	51,201	387,476	322,249	65,227	15,561	309	15,252	1,843	1,754	89
1996	846,041	716,109	129,932	475,621	415,159	60,461	355,807	296,856	58,951	10,701	217	10,484	3,912	3,876	36
1997	571,124	462,832	108,292	340,950	286,204	54,746	219,893	175,526	44,367	9,231	84	9,147	1,050	1,018	32
1998	635,583	536,679	98,904	376,537	326,675	49,862	248,937	207,824	41,112	7,916	67	7,849	2,194	2,113	81
1999	592,988	504,693	88,294	350,258	309,442	40,815	235,780	193,604	42,177	5,249	27	5,222	1,700	1,620	80
2000	467,827	391,031	76,796	267,716	232,352	35,364	191,277	156,051	35,226	5,704	7	5,696	3,130	2,621	509
2001	285,780	242,830	42,950	161,520	142,632	18,888	118,057	99,101	18,956	5,032	11	5,022	1,171	1,086	85
2002	294,427	259,069	35,358	167,485	153,037	14,448	120,897	105,402	15,495	4,755	59	4,696	1,290	571	719
2003	278,758	231,445	47,312	158,146	131,325	26,821	113,093	99,669	13,424	7,027	18	7,010	492	433	59
2004	323,573	266,524	57,049	192,764	164,305	28,459	123,625	101,849	21,777	6,770	8	6,763	413	362	51
2005	347,535	291,079	56,457	197,473	168,054	29,419	143,231	122,512	20,719	6,240	5	6,236	591	508	83
2006	655,544	597,495	58,049	463,774	435,857	27,918	174,102	151,459	22,644	7,468	17	7,451	10,199	10,163	37
Total[a]	6,103,308	5,172,146	931,162	3,551,491	3,113,090	438,402	2,432,176	2,032,102	400,073	91,656	829	90,827	27,985	26,125	1,860
Average[a]	508,609	431,012	77,597	295,958	259,424	36,533	202,681	169,342	33,339	7,638	69	7,569	2,332	2,177	155

[a] The years 1995 to 2006 were used for total and average volume harvested.

Table A.8—Timber cut and sold on Alabama national forests, 1990 to 2006

Year	Volume		Value	
	thousand board feet	thousand cubic feet	dollars	dollars per thousand board feet
1990	74,942	13,626	5,067,595.32	67.62
1991	79,638	14,480	4,824,142.85	60.58
1992	103,810	18,874	6,806,887.96	65.57
1993	70,987	12,907	5,189,259.98	73.10
1994	53,548	9,736	4,773,504.86	89.15
1995	60,223	10,950	5,498,316.87	91.30
1996	65,027	11,823	8,046,913.00	123.75
1997	31,364	5,703	3,843,132.31	122.53
1998	32,694	5,944	4,308,200.52	131.77
1999	19,419	3,531	2,398,262.73	123.50
2000	19,550	3,555	2,336,626.87	119.52
2001	20,298	3,691	1,679,475.03	82.74
2002	10,656	1,938	736,068.65	69.08
2003	3,956	719	320,471.16	81.02
2004	7,947	1,472	863,800.31	108.70
2005	13,138	2,627	897,945.79	68.35
2006	15,460	3,092	1,336,247.33	86.43
Total[a]	299,732	55,044	32,265,460.57	
Average[a]	24,978	4,587	2,688,788.38	100.72

[a] The years 1995 to 2006 were used for total and average volume harvested.

Table A.9—Timber cut and sold on Arkansas national forests, 1990 to 2006

Year	Volume		Value	
	thousand board feet	thousand cubic feet	dollars	dollars per thousand board feet
1990	189,033	34,370	16,041,737.38	84.86
1991	139,483	25,361	11,298,480.95	81.00
1992	95,812	17,420	9,439,024.52	98.52
1993	131,214	23,857	12,556,230.46	95.69
1994	146,108	26,565	16,145,428.13	110.50
1995	151,400	27,598	18,085,184.88	119.45
1996	176,959	32,257	23,867,251.03	134.87
1997	141,986	25,882	23,371,418.60	164.60
1998	152,439	27,787	26,310,544.44	172.60
1999	168,566	30,727	32,862,810.53	194.95
2000	150,687	27,468	29,933,810.13	198.65
2001	110,017	20,004	15,909,282.13	144.61
2002	104,144	18,937	14,218,125.06	136.52
2003	114,319	20,839	15,711,021.92	137.43
2004	112,005	20,417	11,623,133.56	103.77
2005	121,620	22,673	15,535,199.81	127.74
2006	122,022	23,293	14,678,471.50	120.29
Total[a]	1,626,163	297,882	242,106,253.59	
Average[a]	135,514	24,824	20,175,521.13	146.29

[a] The years 1995 to 2006 were used for total and average volume harvested.

Table A.10—Timber cut and sold on Florida national forests, 1990 to 2006

Year	Volume		Value	
	thousand board feet	*thousand cubic feet*	*dollars*	*dollars per thousand board feet*
1990	86,559	15,738	6,328,970.83	73.12
1991	58,014	10,548	4,179,998.36	72.05
1992	75,747	13,772	4,902,592.64	64.72
1993	90,121	16,386	5,464,724.88	60.64
1994	58,448	10,627	3,372,184.09	57.70
1995	65,473	11,902	4,306,776.08	65.78
1996	35,830	6,513	3,329,575.59	92.93
1997	32,295	5,871	3,146,318.11	97.42
1998	51,229	9,313	4,801,931.60	93.73
1999	26,148	4,753	2,188,262.47	83.69
2000	33,243	6,043	3,491,450.54	105.03
2001	25,345	4,608	2,598,880.80	102.54
2002	27,065	4,921	1,880,848.34	69.49
2003	41,747	7,590	2,109,704.08	50.54
2004	13,308	2,526	1,217,680.50	91.50
2005	37,868	7,559	1,409,377.76	37.22
2006	38,009	7,553	2,728,315.59	71.78
Total[a]	427,561	79,152	33,209,121.46	
Average[a]	35,630	6,596	2,767,426.79	80.14

[a] The years 1995 to 2006 were used for total and average volume harvested.

Table A.11—Timber cut and sold on Georgia national forests, 1990 to 2006

Year	Volume		Value	
	thousand board feet	*thousand cubic feet*	*dollars*	*dollars per thousand board feet*
1990	53,650	9,754	3,128,877.59	58.32
1991	52,116	9,476	3,797,096.59	72.86
1992	57,755	10,501	4,369,671.75	75.66
1993	54,446	9,899	4,439,644.18	81.54
1994	40,535	7,370	3,204,390.37	79.05
1995	28,348	5,154	2,654,177.27	93.63
1996	40,006	7,274	3,100,884.44	77.51
1997	27,089	4,925	2,366,500.52	87.36
1998	13,750	2,749	1,012,180.02	73.61
1999	9,263	1,852	964,417.39	104.11
2000	748	150	87,138.13	116.47
2001	1,006	183	32,676.00	32.47
2002	638	116	12,847.94	20.15
2003	1,479	274	55,011.15	37.18
2004	1,434	286	114,906.97	80.12
2005	3,264	653	302,849.14	92.78
2006	4,280	856	383,821.39	89.68
Total[a]	131,306	24,472	11,087,410.36	
Average[a]	10,942	2,039	923,950.86	75.42

[a] The years 1995 to 2006 were used for total and average volume harvested.

Table A.12—Timber cut and sold on Kentucky national forests, 1990 to 2006

Year	Volume		Value	
	thousand board feet	thousand cubic feet	dollars	dollars per thousand board feet
1990	29,705	5,401	1,167,038.30	39.29
1991	39,632	7,206	1,633,999.67	41.23
1992	38,293	6,962	1,655,733.77	43.24
1993	38,413	6,984	1,908,476.73	49.68
1994	20,813	3,784	1,370,326.78	65.84
1995	12,162	2,211	960,831.40	79.01
1996	19,754	3,592	1,500,314.84	75.95
1997	16,734	3,043	1,462,565.44	87.40
1998	9,431	1,715	770,235.71	81.67
1999	1,549	282	102,611.26	66.25
2000	1,998	363	111,023.40	55.58
2001	4,063	739	151,451.03	37.28
2002	2,005	369	74,833.40	37.31
2003	3,878	709	294,027.73	75.81
2004	2,646	479	185,160.01	69.99
2005	1,628	279	87,332.38	53.66
2006	1,047	186	29,035.23	27.73
Total[a]	76,894	13,965	5,729,421.83	
Average[a]	6,408	1,164	477,451.82	62.30

[a] The years 1995 to 2006 were used for total and average volume harvested.

Table A.13—Timber cut and sold on Louisiana national forests, 1990 to 2006

Year	Volume		Value	
	thousand board feet	thousand cubic feet	dollars	dollars per thousand board feet
1990	155,977	28,359	11,710,951.36	75.08
1991	122,035	22,188	9,993,670.29	81.89
1992	142,680	25,942	13,108,093.78	91.87
1993	81,688	14,852	8,821,436.51	107.99
1994	81,473	14,813	9,223,225.73	113.21
1995	64,283	11,278	7,497,680.81	116.64
1996	72,379	12,698	9,607,439.57	132.74
1997	56,609	9,931	10,642,780.21	188.00
1998	48,547	8,517	7,761,088.33	159.87
1999	46,720	8,197	8,403,109.39	179.86
2000	29,660	5,203	5,391,862.72	181.79
2001	17,246	3,136	2,150,962.48	124.73
2002	28,013	5,090	3,764,325.52	134.38
2003	8,695	1,581	1,591,028.51	182.98
2004	28,645	5,227	4,232,066.74	147.74
2005	24,114	4,523	2,693,843.98	111.71
2006	40,320	7,849	4,128,987.10	102.41
Total[a]	465,232	83,230	67,865,175.36	
Average[a]	38,769	6,936	5,655,431.28	146.90

[a] The years 1995 to 2006 were used for total and average volume harvested.

Table A.14—Timber cut and sold on Mississippi national forests, 1990 to 2006

Year	Volume		Value	
	thousand board feet	*thousand cubic feet*	*dollars*	*dollars per thousand board feet*
1990	229,199	41,673	21,594,265.68	94.22
1991	222,821	40,513	18,844,046.22	84.57
1992	206,417	37,530	20,961,158.87	101.55
1993	204,459	37,174	21,653,066.64	105.90
1994	176,319	32,058	21,630,804.35	122.68
1995	193,461	37,712	27,144,509.31	140.31
1996	210,252	40,985	29,414,158.03	139.90
1997	101,193	19,726	18,307,616.31	180.92
1998	112,748	21,978	18,728,291.89	166.11
1999	154,777	30,171	27,706,292.29	179.01
2000	129,600	25,263	25,185,654.71	194.33
2001	40,471	7,359	7,331,252.50	181.15
2002	37,225	6,767	6,015,561.53	161.60
2003	33,293	6,173	6,118,859.38	183.79
2004	60,321	11,209	9,633,884.85	159.71
2005	61,465	11,908	8,225,527.65	133.82
2006	292,621	58,388	21,540,051.04	73.61
Total[a]	1,427,429	277,638	205,351,659.49	
Average[a]	118,952	23,136	17,112,638.29	157.85

[a] The years 1995 to 2006 were used for total and average volume harvested.

Table A.15—Timber cut and sold on North Carolina national forests, 1990 to 2006

Year	Volume		Value	
	thousand board feet	*thousand cubic feet*	*dollars*	*dollars per thousand board feet*
1990	71,055	12,919	1,463,305.53	20.59
1991	55,996	10,181	1,204,632.01	21.51
1992	69,717	12,676	1,854,165.80	26.60
1993	50,675	9,214	2,007,153.55	39.61
1994	36,803	6,691	1,430,761.50	38.88
1995	37,913	6,893	2,370,285.23	62.52
1996	30,550	5,555	1,824,041.26	59.71
1997	24,459	4,447	1,979,965.60	80.95
1998	26,141	4,753	1,895,139.10	72.50
1999	26,096	4,745	2,260,469.09	86.62
2000	18,574	3,377	1,257,016.86	67.68
2001	10,196	1,854	768,921.31	75.42
2002	13,471	2,449	544,674.56	40.43
2003	7,750	1,407	481,333.29	62.10
2004	14,621	2,652	1,255,583.51	85.88
2005	9,373	1,722	864,414.12	92.23
2006	14,155	2,662	1,326,829.87	93.74
Total[a]	233,298	42,516	16,828,673.80	
Average[a]	19,441	3,543	1,402,389.48	73.31

[a] The years 1995 to 2006 were used for total and average volume harvested.

Table A.16—Timber cut and sold on Oklahoma national forests, 1990 to 2006

Year	Volume		Value	
	thousand board feet	*thousand cubic feet*	*dollars*	*dollars per thousand board feet*
1990	25,109	4,565	1,653,805.68	65.87
1991	29,738	5,407	2,167,675.04	72.89
1992	13,490	2,453	846,502.22	62.75
1993	21,480	3,906	1,648,254.35	76.73
1994	19,096	3,472	2,309,219.10	120.92
1995	17,561	3,193	2,185,718.19	124.46
1996	21,208	3,856	3,633,683.56	171.33
1997	19,056	3,465	3,437,835.30	180.41
1998	11,170	2,031	1,973,199.70	176.66
1999	15,508	2,820	3,047,267.50	196.50
2000	7,593	1,381	1,333,955.33	175.68
2001	4,102	746	531,426.07	129.56
2002	10,838	1,971	1,394,485.86	128.67
2003	9,360	1,702	1,245,046.85	133.02
2004	16,100	2,927	2,623,671.40	162.96
2005	11,746	2,209	1,588,899.26	135.27
2006	14,420	2,810	1,548,433.77	107.38
Total[a]	158,662	29,109	24,543,622.79	
Average[a]	13,222	2,426	2,045,301.90	151.82

[a] The years 1995 to 2006 were used for total and average volume harvested.

Table A.17—Timber cut and sold on South Carolina national forests, 1990 to 2006

Year	Volume		Value	
	thousand board feet	*thousand cubic feet*	*dollars*	*dollars per thousand board feet*
1990	318,551	57,918	13,169,076.34	41.34
1991	74,418	13,530	4,112,392.30	55.26
1992	72,082	13,106	6,316,649.37	87.63
1993	65,952	11,991	5,650,337.58	85.67
1994	58,962	10,720	5,890,001.57	99.89
1995	40,422	7,349	4,337,908.67	107.32
1996	37,292	6,780	4,157,306.00	111.48
1997	38,930	7,078	5,310,660.11	136.41
1998	18,609	3,383	2,052,043.77	110.27
1999	53,205	9,674	6,215,632.90	116.82
2000	30,253	5,500	4,146,789.73	137.07
2001	22,527	4,096	3,005,038.30	133.40
2002	19,445	3,536	2,031,949.42	104.50
2003	15,243	2,772	2,480,159.03	162.71
2004	26,819	4,888	2,838,972.96	105.86
2005	15,438	2,902	1,828,343.85	118.43
2006	35,534	7,065	2,465,442.98	69.38
Total[a]	353,716	65,024	40,870,247.72	
Average[a]	29,476	5,419	3,405,853.98	117.80

[a] The years 1995 to 2006 were used for total and average volume harvested.

Table A.18 — Timber cut and sold on Tennessee national forests, 1990 to 2006

Year	Volume		Value	
	thousand board feet	*thousand cubic feet*	*dollars*	*dollars per thousand board feet*
1990	30,459	5,538	1,402,529.84	46.05
1991	25,073	4,559	966,658.50	38.55
1992	31,535	5,734	1,320,164.42	41.86
1993	29,455	5,355	1,443,334.00	49.00
1994	21,120	3,840	1,070,699.34	50.70
1995	17,646	3,208	1,104,127.42	62.57
1996	11,552	2,100	792,069.72	68.57
1997	14,174	2,577	1,249,261.38	88.14
1998	12,368	2,249	1,089,671.98	88.11
1999	17,443	3,171	1,696,486.13	97.26
2000	12,190	2,216	1,184,651.43	97.19
2001	5,750	1,274	442,455.55	76.95
2002	2,760	502	90,110.46	32.65
2003	3,570	659	298,297.61	83.55
2004	1,826	342	119,244.37	65.30
2005	5,599	1,092	807,363.80	144.20
2006	4,101	767	667,591.61	162.80
Total[a]	108,978	20,159	9,541,331.46	
Average[a]	9,081	1,680	795,110.96	88.94

[a] The years 1995 to 2006 were used for total and average volume harvested.

Table A.19 — Timber cut and sold on Texas national forests, 1990 to 2006

Year	Volume		Value	
	thousand board feet	*thousand cubic feet*	*dollars*	*dollars per thousand board feet*
1990	95,471	17,358	7,938,604.98	83.15
1991	61,536	11,188	7,103,757.43	115.44
1992	100,611	18,293	12,726,145.91	126.49
1993	81,917	14,894	11,284,732.71	137.76
1994	93,750	17,045	14,357,370.94	153.15
1995	65,313	11,875	10,571,472.26	161.86
1996	88,959	16,174	16,045,258.54	180.37
1997	39,168	7,122	7,794,231.35	198.99
1998	118,164	21,484	19,261,740.90	163.01
1999	28,385	5,161	6,053,135.78	213.25
2000	11,262	2,048	2,236,089.18	198.56
2001	6,754	1,228	1,240,533.57	183.68
2002	22,872	4,159	3,664,492.36	160.21
2003	21,046	3,827	3,190,809.06	151.61
2004	22,986	4,184	3,772,632.46	164.13
2005	24,722	4,615	4,135,221.26	167.27
2006	58,773	11,588	6,102,449.88	103.83
Total[a]	508,405	93,464	84,068,066.60	
Average[a]	42,367	7,789	7,005,672.22	170.56

[a] The years 1995 to 2006 were used for total and average volume harvested.

Table A.20—Timber cut and sold on Virginia national forests, 1990 to 2006

Year	Volume		Value	
	thousand board feet	*thousand cubic feet*	*dollars*	*dollars per thousand board feet*
1990	58,458	10,629	935,226.46	16.00
1991	64,736	11,770	1,359,641.02	21.00
1992	53,530	9,733	1,376,736.46	25.72
1993	56,244	10,226	1,999,480.76	35.55
1994	53,245	9,681	2,623,805.77	49.28
1995	49,924	9,077	3,125,306.77	62.60
1996	36,274	6,595	2,998,446.10	82.66
1997	28,067	5,103	2,777,463.60	98.96
1998	28,292	5,144	2,557,913.66	90.41
1999	25,907	4,710	2,614,041.09	100.90
2000	22,471	4,086	2,260,905.34	100.61
2001	18,006	3,274	1,689,116.27	93.81
2002	15,294	2,781	1,503,497.23	98.31
2003	13,791	2,508	1,363,815.58	98.90
2004	14,916	2,755	1,354,896.61	90.84
2005	17,561	3,361	1,513,024.28	86.16
2006	14,803	2,933	1,060,725.65	71.66
Total[a]	285,304	52,328	24,819,152.18	
Average[a]	23,775	4,361	2,068,262.68	89.65

[a] The years 1995 to 2006 were used for total and average volume harvested.

Table A.21—All-live removals by State, utilization, and species group, all owners, 1995 to 2006

State	Utilization and species group								
	Utilized			Nonutilized			Total		
	Soft-wood	Hard-wood	Total	Soft-wood	Hard-wood	Total	Soft-wood	Hard-wood	Total
	thousand cubic feet								
Alabama	879,452	380,046	1,259,498	27,510	47,651	75,161	906,962	427,697	1,334,659
Arkansas	516,174	228,743	744,917	47,154	111,578	158,732	563,328	340,321	903,649
Florida	413,018	68,305	481,323	44,886	54,288	99,174	457,904	122,593	580,497
Georgia	1,110,984	288,329	1,399,313	55,111	107,576	162,687	1,166,095	395,905	1,562,000
Kentucky	10,264	180,486	190,750	13,036	115,814	128,850	23,300	296,300	319,600
Louisiana	610,205	265,373	875,578	54,832	73,396	128,228	665,037	338,769	1,003,806
Mississippi	603,044	392,503	995,547	28,984	59,617	88,601	632,028	452,120	1,084,148
North Carolina	640,410	410,853	1,051,263	59,986	161,315	221,301	700,396	572,168	1,272,564
Oklahoma	80,041	35,526	115,567	14,685	36,390	51,075	94,726	71,916	166,642
South Carolina	559,562	188,907	748,469	36,547	28,786	65,333	596,109	217,693	813,802
Tennessee	130,887	275,694	406,581	15,962	136,622	152,584	146,849	412,316	559,165
Texas	525,248	115,785	641,033	23,766	65,907	89,673	549,014	181,692	730,706
Virginia	313,339	364,039	677,378	27,225	122,952	150,177	340,564	486,991	827,555
Total	6,392,628	3,194,589	9,587,217	449,684	1,121,892	1,571,576	6,842,312	4,316,481	11,158,793

Table A.22—All-live removals by State, utilization, and species group, national forests, 1995 to 2006

	Utilization and species group														
	Utilized			Nonutilized			Nonutilized (logging residue)			Nonutilized (other residue)			Total		
State	Soft-wood	Hard-wood	Total	Soft-wood	Hard-wood	Total	Soft-wood	Hard-wood	Total	Soft-wood	Hard-wood	Total	Soft-wood	Hard-wood	Total
	thousand cubic feet														
Alabama	3,849	500	4,349	5,974	3,528	9,502	139	200	339	5,835	3,328	9,163	9,823	4,028	13,851
Arkansas	19,095	4,517	23,612	8,936	8,669	17,605	4,501	3,111	7,612	4,435	5,558	9,993	28,031	13,186	41,217
Florida	8,689	0	8,689	1,968	646	2,614	111	0	111	1,857	646	2,503	10,657	646	11,303
Georgia	1,581	209	1,790	88	6,361	6,449	88	0	88	0	6,361	6,361	1,669	6,570	8,239
Kentucky	190	3,000	3,190	10	1,100	1,110	1	200	201	9	900	909	200	4,100	4,300
Louisiana	5,256	766	6,022	4,088	3,121	7,209	389	0	389	3,699	3,121	6,820	9,344	3,887	13,231
Mississippi	31,669	7,168	38,837	1,987	1,397	3,384	1,136	1,078	2,214	851	319	1,170	33,656	8,565	42,221
North Carolina	0	0	0	366	2,232	2,598	366	2,192	2,558	0	40	40	366	2,232	2,598
Oklahoma	2,000	0	2,000	100	0	100	10	0	10	90	0	90	2,100	0	2,100
South Carolina	2,788	0	2,788	13	0	13	13	0	13	0	0	0	2,801	0	2,801
Tennessee	4,785	0	4,785	890	9,230	10,120	0	155	155	890	9,075	9,965	5,675	9,230	14,905
Texas	534	0	534	0	0	0	0	0	0	0	0	0	534	0	534
Virginia	0	12,652	12,652	154	8,837	8,991	0	591	591	154	8,246	8,400	154	21,489	21,643
Total	80,436	28,812	109,248	24,574	45,121	69,695	6,754	7,527	14,281	17,820	37,594	55,414	105,010	73,933	178,943
Adjustment for under utilization	77,218	25,066	102,284	27,792	48,867	76,659	9,972	11,273	21,245	17,820	37,594	55,414	105,010	73,933	178,943

Table A.23—All-live removals by State, utilization, and species group, other public, 1995 to 2006

	Utilization and species group								
	Utilized			Nonutilized			Total		
State	Soft-wood	Hard-wood	Total	Soft-wood	Hard-wood	Total	Soft-wood	Hard-wood	Total
	thousand cubic feet								
Alabama	13,269	5,074	18,343	1,773	6,302	8,075	15,042	11,376	26,418
Arkansas	4,067	7,409	11,476	1,824	20,421	22,245	5,891	27,830	33,721
Florida	47,767	1,265	49,032	15,200	17,522	32,722	62,967	18,787	81,754
Georgia	38,098	9,536	47,634	6,430	7,985	14,415	44,528	17,521	62,049
Kentucky	0	1,827	1,827	0	1,173	1,173	0	3,000	3,000
Louisiana	4,789	7,076	11,865	356	11,945	12,301	5,145	19,021	24,166
Mississippi	16,804	4,944	21,748	3,740	8,505	12,245	20,544	13,449	33,993
North Carolina	10,767	885	11,652	710	510	1,220	11,477	1,395	12,872
Oklahoma	701	326	1,027	500	174	674	1,201	500	1,701
South Carolina	30,791	2,999	33,790	1,625	1,186	2,811	32,416	4,185	36,601
Tennessee	5,821	2,855	8,676	7,102	62,301	69,403	12,923	65,156	78,079
Texas	561	0	561	0	0	0	561	0	561
Virginia	4,430	21,164	25,594	133	9,811	9,944	4,563	30,975	35,538
Total	177,865	65,360	243,225	39,393	147,835	187,228	217,258	213,195	430,453

Table A.24—All-live removals by State, utilization, and species group, forest industry, 1995 to 2006

| | Utilization and species group | | | | | | | | |
| | Utilized | | | Nonutilized | | | Total | | |
State	Soft-wood	Hard-wood	Total	Soft-wood	Hard-wood	Total	Soft-wood	Hard-wood	Total
	thousand cubic feet								
Alabama	226,611	59,598	286,209	2,339	4,425	6,764	228,950	64,023	292,973
Arkansas	286,669	50,267	336,936	13,891	17,138	31,029	300,560	67,405	367,965
Florida	85,340	7,621	92,961	2,382	1,341	3,723	87,722	8,962	96,684
Georgia	313,754	21,721	335,475	1,328	3,772	5,100	315,082	25,493	340,575
Kentucky	185	5,760	5,945	15	640	655	200	6,400	6,600
Louisiana	294,811	74,699	369,510	19,263	9,629	28,892	314,074	84,328	398,402
Mississippi	116,384	37,949	154,333	1,865	3,900	5,765	118,249	41,849	160,098
North Carolina	148,572	31,778	180,350	1,185	334	1,519	149,757	32,112	181,869
Oklahoma	60,766	11,013	71,779	4,720	11,288	16,008	65,486	22,301	87,787
South Carolina	144,572	21,524	166,096	8,162	674	8,836	152,734	22,198	174,932
Tennessee	37,470	19,216	56,686	467	3,054	3,521	37,937	22,270	60,207
Texas	210,417	17,919	228,336	6,153	6,134	12,287	216,570	24,053	240,623
Virginia	43,951	14,912	58,863	3,008	3,125	6,133	46,959	18,037	64,996
Total	1,969,502	373,977	2,343,479	64,778	65,454	130,232	2,034,280	439,431	2,473,711

Table A.25—All-live removals by State, utilization, and species group, nonindustrial private forest, 1995 to 2006

| | Utilization and species group | | | | | | | | |
| | Utilized | | | Nonutilized | | | Total | | |
State	Soft-wood	Hard-wood	Total	Soft-wood	Hard-wood	Total	Soft-wood	Hard-wood	Total
	thousand cubic feet								
Alabama	635,722	314,874	950,596	17,424	33,396	50,820	653,146	348,270	1,001,416
Arkansas	206,342	166,551	372,893	22,503	65,349	87,852	228,845	231,900	460,745
Florida	271,221	59,420	330,641	25,337	34,779	60,116	296,558	94,199	390,757
Georgia	757,551	256,862	1,014,413	47,265	89,459	136,724	804,816	346,321	1,151,137
Kentucky	9,889	169,899	179,788	13,011	112,901	125,912	22,900	282,800	305,700
Louisiana	305,349	182,832	488,181	31,124	48,701	79,825	336,473	231,533	568,006
Mississippi	438,187	342,442	780,629	21,393	45,815	67,208	459,580	388,257	847,837
North Carolina	481,070	378,190	859,260	57,725	158,239	215,964	538,795	536,429	1,075,224
Oklahoma	16,574	24,513	41,087	9,365	24,592	33,957	25,939	49,105	75,044
South Carolina	381,411	164,384	545,795	26,746	26,926	53,672	408,157	191,310	599,467
Tennessee	82,811	253,624	336,435	7,503	62,038	69,541	90,314	315,662	405,976
Texas	313,736	97,866	411,602	17,613	59,773	77,386	331,349	157,639	488,988
Virginia	264,957	315,311	580,268	23,930	101,179	125,109	288,887	416,490	705,377
Total	4,164,820	2,726,768	6,891,588	320,939	863,147	1,184,086	4,485,759	3,589,915	8,075,674

www.ingramcontent.com/pod-product-compliance
Lightning Source LLC
Chambersburg PA
CBHW081136280526
45787CB00007B/3111